The Transcontinental
RAILROAD

Using Proportions to Solve Problems

Therese Shea

PowerMath™

The Rosen Publishing Group's
PowerKids Press™
New York

Published in 2007 by The Rosen Publishing Group, Inc.
29 East 21st Street, New York, NY 10010

Book Design: Daniel Hosek

Library of Congress Cataloging-in-Publication Data

Shea, Therese.
  The transcontinental railroad : using proportions to solve problems / Therese Shea.
      p. cm.—(Math for the real world)
  Includes index.
  ISBN 1-4042-3361-X (library binding)
  ISBN 1-4042-6075-7 (pbk.)
  6-pack ISBN 1-4042-6076-5
  1. Ratio and proportion—Juvenile literature. 2. Problem solving—Juvenile literature. 3. Railroads—United States–History—Juvenile literature. 4. Union Pacific Railroad Company—History—Juvenile literature. 5. Central Pacific Railroad Company—History—Juvenile literature. I. Title. II. Series.

  QA117.S54 2006
  513.2'4--dc22

                              2005015160

Manufactured in the United States of America

CONTENTS

NEW IDEAS FOR A GROWING COUNTRY

Following the discovery of gold near Sacramento, California, in 1848, many people began to move to the western lands of the United States, signaling the start of the California gold rush. People traveled from faraway places in search of wealth, land, and new lives.

By the mid-1850s, travelers from the East could take a train to the end of the line: Omaha, Nebraska. From there, some traveled the remainder of the way through dangerous lands by **stagecoach**. Others went by wagon on the Oregon and California trails. Wagons could travel 15 miles (24 km) on a good day. Other travelers sailed around the tip of South America. Still others sailed to the **Isthmus** of Panama, walked through the jungle, and sailed up the west coast. All these routes took a great amount of time. By land, the trip could take 6 months. A lot of things could and did go wrong. Wagons broke down. Sickness was common, especially on the route that crossed the Isthmus of Panama.

People began to look for a better form of transportation to cross the continent. They believed a transcontinental railroad that spanned the entire continent could be the answer. In this book, we will learn about the building of this railroad. We will also learn how to use proportions to solve problems while examining the obstacles that were overcome to complete the first transcontinental railroad.

This map shows the Oregon and California trails. Before the transcontinental railroad, travelers had to travel these trails by wagon or on horseback, which took several months.

...vagons could travel about 15 miles
...1 day, how many days would it take
...em to travel from St. Joseph to Ft.
...ramie, a distance of approximately
...0 miles? Round your answer to the
...arest whole day.

...solve this problem, first set up the
...oportion: $\dfrac{\text{miles}}{\text{days}} = \dfrac{\text{miles}}{\text{days}}$

Cross multiply to set up an algebraic **equation**.
Then divide to solve for d.

Let d = days $\dfrac{15}{1} = \dfrac{700}{d}$

$$15\,d = 700$$

$$d = 46.6$$

It would take about 47 days to travel 700 miles.

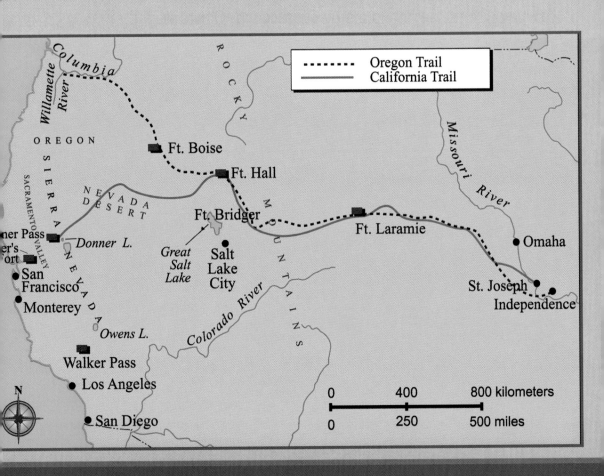

- - - - - - - Oregon Trail
———————— California Trail

Columbia

Willamette River

R O C K Y

Missouri River

OREGON

Ft. Boise

SIERRA   Ft. Hall

SACRAMENTO

NEVADA
DESERT

Ft. Bridger

Ft. Laramie

M
O
U
N
T
A
I
N
S

Omaha

...ner Pass
...er's
...ort

Donner L.

Great
Salt
Lake

Salt
Lake
City

N
E
V
A
D
A

San
Francisco

Monterey

Owens L.

Colorado River

St. Joseph

Independence

Walker Pass

Los Angeles

N

0   400   800 kilometers

0   250   500 miles

San Diego

5

EARLY TRAINS

In 1804, an English inventor named Richard Trevithick created the first railway steam **locomotive**. In the 1820s, engineers in the United States began to construct locomotives to pull railroad cars. Peter Cooper invented the compact steam engine, which was much smaller than other engines being built. To prove that his steam engine was efficient, he organized a race between his engine, called the Tom Thumb, and a horse-drawn railroad car. The Tom Thumb beat the horse for most of the race before a problem caused the engine to break down. Cooper's steam engine traveled about 15 miles (24 km) per hour. Early locomotives like this one sparked many people's interest and imagination.

However, early trains were uncomfortable and not very safe. Most passenger train cars were open, so that passengers experienced the outside weather. Animals on the track often caused accidents. The brakes had to be pulled by hand by a brakeman on the train. It was common for trains to tip over as they rounded curves.

Regardless of their drawbacks, trains made it easier for people to ship goods and travel long distances. Improvements were made over time. The amount of track grew quickly from 762 miles (1,226 km) in 1834, to 4,311 miles (6,936 km) in 1844, to about 15,675 miles (25,221 km) in 1854!

Early trains, like the Tom Thumb and passenger car shown here, could often travel only on certain tracks because companies built the tracks using different measurements between rails. It would take many years before the companies agreed on 4 feet 8.5 inches (1.44 m) as the standard measurement.

Between 1844 and 1854 there were 11,364 miles of track built. At this rate, approximately how many miles of track were built per year?

To solve this problem, we need to find out the number of years between 1844 and 1854. 1854–1844 = 10 years

Start by setting up the proportion: $\dfrac{\text{miles}}{\text{years}} = \dfrac{\text{miles}}{\text{years}}$

Let x = amount of track built $\dfrac{11,364}{10} = \dfrac{x}{1}$

$$11,364 = 10x$$

$$x = 1,136.4 \text{ miles per year}$$

At this rate, approximately 1,136.4 miles of track were built per year.

COOPER'S "TOM THUMB" 1829–30 BALTIMORE & OHIO R. R.

In 1832, a newspaper reporter first suggested a transcontinental railroad. At that time, few thought such an achievement was possible. However, as the United States territory expanded and more people sought routes west, the government began to think it was needed.

In 1853, just a few years after the beginning of the gold rush, Congress approved a plan to have people explore and map the best routes for a railroad track across the continent. Secretary of War Jefferson Davis oversaw the Pacific Railroad surveys, which were official explorations of western routes. Several different paths were discussed, but none were approved. At this time, the U.S. government, like the rest of the nation, was filled with conflict about the issue of slavery. Southern states wanted to keep slavery to sustain their agricultural economy. Northern states wanted to abolish slavery and feared a southern railroad route would spread slavery into the new western territories. Each side wanted the railroad route to run through its states. The railroad became a symbol of the power struggle. The 2 sides could not agree, so nothing was done. However, the path of the route would remain in the minds of 2 men who would eventually transform the nation's transportation system.

This map of the United States, made in 1859, shows existing rail lines and proposed routes for a transcontinental railroad.

Grenville Dodge had worked on railroads from the time he was a young boy. In 1853, he conducted a survey for the Mississippi and Missouri Railroad looking for a transcontinental route that would cross Iowa and follow the Platte River valley. Thomas Durant, a businessman, and Henry Farnam, a railroad investor, funded his trip. The route Dodge followed was known as the Platte Valley Route. He was not the first to travel this way. Cheyenne and Sioux Indian tribes, a religious group called the **Mormons**, and even some trading companies had used this path. The trail followed the Platte River and wound through the Rocky Mountains. It was ideal for laying railroad track because it was a mostly wide, flat trail. Even with a realistic route, Dodge, Durant, and Farnam had a difficult time convincing others to join them at first.

Theodore Judah had already built part of the Erie Railroad rail system and a small railroad line between Sacramento and Folsom, California, when serious talk of the transcontinental railroad began. Judah wanted to find the best route east from California. The most difficult part of the route would be traveling through the Sierra Nevada mountain range. A friend suggested the Donner Pass and, with that, Judah had a complete route. Collis Huntington, a storekeeper, invested in Judah's scheme and brought in 3 other businessmen who were also interested. These businessmen—Collis Huntington, Leland Stanford, Charles Crocker, and Mark Hopkins—would soon become known as the Big Four for the power they held. The Central Pacific Railroad was born on June 28, 1861, with Stanford as president.

Theodore Judah

Grenville Dodge

eodore Judah (above) went to Washington,
.C., and succeeded in persuading the
vernment to support the railroad. Grenville
dge (right) was involved with construction of
e transcontinental railroad until its completion.

During the 1860 presidential election, the Republican Party pushed the idea that a transcontinental railroad would strengthen the country economically and that the government should help pay for the project. When Republican candidate Abraham Lincoln won the election, the Southern states soon withdrew from the Union. That meant there was no longer a need to consider a southern route. A northern route, which would aid the north in the Civil War, was approved. Also, a telegraph line would be constructed alongside the tracks to ensure communication between the coasts. Lincoln signed the Pacific Railroad Act on July 1, 1862.

This act created the Union Pacific Railroad Company, which would start building tracks west from the Missouri River. At the same time, the Central Pacific would build east from Sacramento, California. For each mile of land, a certain amount of government **bonds** were given to the railroad companies to serve as loans from the federal government. They could be sold to the public to obtain money, but would need to be paid back. The more difficult the land, the more bonds the companies would receive per mile. Track laid on flat land was worth $16,000 per mile. Track laid through the foothills of mountains was worth $32,000 per mile.

When Abraham Lincoln (pictured here) signed the Pacific Railroad Act in 1862, a charter was granted to the Union Pacific Railroad and the Central Pacific Railroad companies giving them permission to build a railroad and telegraph line between Omaha, Nebraska, and the California territory.

Railroad track laid through mountains was worth even more money per mile. If the Central Pacific received bonds worth $336,000 for laying 7 miles of track through the Sierra Nevada, how much was each mile worth?

To solve this problem, first set up the proportion:

$$\frac{\text{dollars}}{\text{miles}} = \frac{\text{dollars}}{\text{miles}}$$

Let t = amount of money per mile

Cross multiply to set up the algebraic equation:

$$\frac{\$336,000}{7} = \frac{t}{1}$$

$$\$336,000 = 7t$$

$$t = 48,000$$

Each mile of track laid through mountains was worth $48,000.

The terms of the Pacific Railroad Act granted the railroad companies 10 square miles (26 sq km) of land for every mile of track laid. The companies were not held responsible for completing a certain amount of track. Instead, the laying of track became a competition about which company could lay the most track. The company that worked the fastest received the largest amount of land and money.

The race was on. The Central Pacific Railroad broke ground on January 8, 1863, in Sacramento with a shovel of dirt dug by Leland Stanford, railroad president and governor of California. Although the Union Pacific began working on December 2, 1863, the Civil War limited its progress for some time.

The men in charge of the railroad companies would stop at nothing to make money for themselves and to make their railroads successful. Before they could collect any bonds and land from the government, they first had to lay 40 miles (64 km) of track. Theodore Judah estimated that 40 miles of track would cost about $2.72 million. At that time, the Central Pacific did not have enough money to pay for these first tracks. To raise money, the railroad tried to sell stocks and bonds to the public, but the public was not buying. The Big Four had to act.

Both the Union Pacific and the Central Pacific railroads would encounter many problems while laying track. This picture shows Cheyenne Indians attacking workers on the transcontinental railroad in 1867.

According to Judah's estimate, how much did each mile (1.6 km) of track cost?

To solve this problem, first set up the proportion: $\dfrac{\text{miles}}{\text{cost}} = \dfrac{\text{miles}}{\text{cost}}$

c = the cost of each mile

$$\dfrac{40}{\$2,720,000} = \dfrac{1}{c}$$

Cross multiply to set up the algebraic equation:
$40 \times c = \$2,720,000$

Divide to solve for c.

$$\dfrac{40 \times c}{40} = \dfrac{\$2,720,000}{40}$$

$$\begin{array}{r} 68,000 \\ 40\overline{)2,720,000} \\ -240 \\ \hline 320 \\ -\;320 \\ \hline 0\,0 \end{array}$$

$c = \$68,000$

Each mile (1.6 km) of track cost $68,000 to lay.

RAILROAD SCHEMES

To secure enough money for Central Pacific Railroad construction, Leland Stanford used his position as governor of California. He received a large amount of money from the state in return for promising to allow the state to use the railroad for its own purposes.

The Big Four devised another scheme to make money. They decided that Charles Crocker would form a construction company, and this company would be hired to lay the track. The Central Pacific paid the construction company whatever price Crocker set. All members of the Big Four owned parts of the construction company and therefore could share in the profits.

Collis Huntington's plan for making money involved the federal government. Through the Pacific Railroad Act, different amounts of money were awarded for laying track through different **terrain**. Huntington asked a geologist to acknowledge that the Sierra Nevada started in the Sacramento Valley, some distance before the mountains actually began. Therefore, the company earned $48,000 for each mile (1.6 km) of track laid in this terrain instead of the $16,000 that was the usual amount earned for each mile of track laid on flat land.

Mark Hopkins

When the lawfulness of the Big Four's money deals was questioned in 1873, Mark Hopkins burned the financial books. ►

Collis Huntington

Charles Crocker

Leland Stanford

The Central Pacific earned $1,152,000 for the miles of "mountain" track they laid before they reached the mountains. How many miles of track did the workers lay?

To solve this problem, first set up the proportion:

$$\frac{\text{dollars}}{\text{miles}} = \frac{\text{dollars}}{\text{miles}}$$

Let r = the number of miles

$$\frac{\$48,000}{1} = \frac{\$1,152,000}{r}$$

Cross multiply to set up the algebraic equation:
$\$48,000 \times r = \$1,152,000$

In a division problem in which numbers with many zeroes are being divided, you can cross an equal number of zeroes off each number. (This is the same as dividing both numbers by the same number, creating a fraction equal to the original.) Then divide the remaining numbers.

```
        24
48) 1,152
   - 96
     192
   - 192
       0
```

r = 24 miles

The Central Pacific workers laid 24 miles of track.

Theodore Judah, who had worked so hard to make his dream of a transcontinental railroad come true, was disappointed by the Big Four's financial schemes. He was afraid they would **bankrupt** the company. He traveled to New York from California to find investors who would buy the Central Pacific from the Big Four. Before he could accomplish his mission, he died in New York of yellow fever, a disease he caught while traveling through Panama.

Meanwhile, the Union Pacific had come up with ways of raising money as well. Early buyers of the company's stock included 3 powerful men. One was Brigham Young, the leader of the Mormons, who hoped his stock would bring more wealth to his community in Utah. The other 2 men were Thomas Durant, who had first financed Grenville Dodge, and George Francis Train, a businessman who had worked with Durant before. Durant and Train bought a small business and turned it into a construction company named Crédit Mobilier of America. This company had all the contracts to lay the Union Pacific track. The company then bought railroad stock and sold it at a much higher price to the public. Durant and Train benefited greatly from this arrangement, while the Union Pacific Railroad acquired enough money to lay hundreds of miles of track.

Durant and Train came up with the Crédit Mobilier scheme to make money on selling railroad stocks.

Thomas Durant

The construction company Crédit Mobilier of America purchased railroad stock for $30,000 per mile of track. They then sold the stock to the public for $50,000 per mile of track. What percent of the original price was Crédit Mobilier's profit?

To solve this problem, first write a sentence to show what you are solving: What percent of the original price was the profit?

original price: $30,000   profit: $50,000 − 30,000 = $20,000

_____ % of $30,000 is $20,000.   Let x = the percent

Set up the proportion and solve for x:

$$\frac{x}{100} = \frac{20,000}{30,000}$$

$$\frac{x}{100} = \frac{2}{3}$$

$3x = 200$

$x = 66\frac{2}{3}\%$

Crédit Mobilier of America sold railroad stock for a $66\frac{2}{3}\%$ profit.

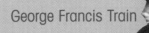

George Francis Train

THE WORKERS

Lincoln signed the Pacific Railroad Act of 1864 to help pull the railroad companies out of dangerous financial situations. The schemes of the Central Pacific and Union Pacific had kept them in constant danger of bankruptcy. This act provided the companies with twice the land grants previously offered and also gave them rights to the minerals found on the land. The companies could sell their own bonds to the public as well.

The railroad companies employed thousands of workers. Many workers were assigned to perform 1 specific job in a series of jobs similar to the way an **assembly line** works. First, the surveyors would mark the spots where the track would be laid. Then, other men would clear the way of trees, soil, and rock. In mountainous terrain, workers would use explosives to blast the rock and form tunnels. Then, other men would step in to lay down railroad ties, the long pieces of wood that hold the rails. The number of ties per mile (1.6 km) varied according to the terrain. In mountainous areas, ties were placed closer together. The average number of ties per mile (1.6 km) was about 2,400 ties. They were spaced about 1.6 feet (0.49 m) apart.

Next came the iron rails. Since each rail weighed about 700 pounds (318 kg), several men were needed to lift each one and put it in its place. Then the rails were hammered into place with iron spikes.

The life of a railroad worker was a difficult one. The long hours of backbreaking labor often made it difficult for men to continue working on the railroad. Many moved on to other jobs.

20

If 240 rails were laid in an hour, about how many were laid every 30 seconds?

r = number of rails laid every 30 seconds

This problem can be represented by a proportion. Be sure that all measures of times are converted to the same unit.

1 hour = 60 minutes

1 minute = 60 seconds

Therefore, 1 hour = 60 × 60 = 3,600 seconds

$$\frac{rails}{time} = \frac{rails}{time} \qquad \frac{r}{30} = \frac{240}{3,600}$$

$$3,600 \times r = 240 \times 30$$

$$\frac{3,600 \times r}{3,600} = \frac{7,200}{3,600}$$

$$r = \frac{72}{36}$$

$$r = 2 \text{ rails}$$

Two rails were laid every 30 seconds.

The railroad was a steady source of work for those willing to work hard. After the Civil War, young ex-soldiers often found work on the Union Pacific Railroad. Many immigrants, especially Irish, German, and Swedish, traveled west to work the rails. Jack Casement, the man in charge of the Union Pacific labor force, was a former general in the Union army. It was a difficult task keeping the workers in line, as many work camps were filled with con men and thieves. Casement and his brother Daniel commanded the workers' respect.

The Casement gangs, as they were called, worked hard to make money. They sometimes slept in "work trains" that were fitted with bunks and supplies the men needed. The trains traveled along with the men. Workers were sometimes paid $2 for building 1 mile (1.6 km) of track on 1 day. They were offered rewards to work even harder, like $3 for 1.5 miles (2.4 km).

If a worker were paid at a rate of $3 for laying 1.5 miles (2.4 km) of track per day, how much would he earn for laying 2 miles of track in 1 day?

To solve this problem, first set up a proportion: $\dfrac{\text{dollars}}{\text{miles}} = \dfrac{\text{dollars}}{\text{miles}}$

Let d = amount earned

$$\frac{d}{2} = \frac{\$3}{1.5} \qquad 1.5d = \$6$$

$$d = \$4$$

A worker would earn $4 for laying 2 miles of track in 1 day.

"General Jack," as the workers called Jack Casement, ran his teams of workers like a small army. They laid an average of 2 miles (3.2 km) of track per day.

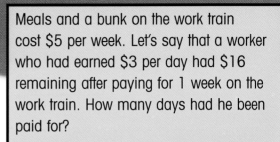

Meals and a bunk on the work train cost $5 per week. Let's say that a worker who had earned $3 per day had $16 remaining after paying for 1 week on the work train. How many days had he been paid for?

d = the number of days

($3 × d) − $5 = $16

First, add 5 to each side.
(3 × d) − 5 + 5 = 16 + 5

3 × d = 21

Then divide both sides by 3.
$$\frac{3 × d}{3} = \frac{21}{3}$$

d = 7 days

The worker had been paid for 7 days.

The Central Pacific had laid about 43 miles (69 km) more track than the Union Pacific by June 1865. However, it was experiencing more problems with its workers than ever before. By this time, the enthusiasm for striking it rich during the gold rush had lessened. However, a new group of pioneers were heading to Nevada, where silver had recently been discovered. Some signed on to work for the Central Pacific as a way to get to the West. They then abandoned the job on the railroad to work in a mine or to work in another business.

Thousands of Chinese immigrants had come to California during the gold rush. The Chinese were **discriminated** against because they wore different clothing and had different religious and cultural traditions. By the 1860s, many of them had not found gold but still had to pay high taxes. The Central Pacific hired a small number of Chinese to fill their shrinking workforce. They were so hardworking and loyal that many more were hired. The Chinese were responsible for aiding the Central Pacific in laying track through the Sierra Nevada mountains. Their knowledge of explosive powders was invaluable in creating tunnels. By 1865, about 6,000 Chinese workers made up 80% of the Central Pacific workforce.

Many Chinese railroad workers lost their lives from working with explosives and also from sicknesses brought on by the bad weather during the Sierra Nevada winters. There were 44 major storms during the winter of 1866–1867 alone.

One tunnel that was 772 feet long required an average of 1.38 kegs of explosive powder per foot of tunnel. About how many kegs of powder were used in all? Round to the nearest whole number.

p = the total number of kegs of powder

To solve this problem, set up a proportion: $\dfrac{feet}{kegs} = \dfrac{feet}{kegs}$

$$\dfrac{1}{1.38} = \dfrac{772}{p}$$

$p = 772 \times 1.38$

```
   7 72
 x 1.38
 ------
 61 76
 231 6
 772
 ------
1,065.36
```

$p = 1,065.36$ kegs

About 1,065 kegs of powder were used to complete the tunnel.

Changing Ways of Life

As the Central Pacific and the Union Pacific raced toward each other, it became clear that life on the land between Omaha, Nebraska, and Sacramento, California, would be changed forever, especially for the Plains Indians. The tracks greatly affected their hunting grounds. The Plains Indians needed a thriving population of buffalo for food, clothing, and materials to make tools and homes. However, the railroad companies believed buffalo were nuisances. Hunters were encouraged to shoot them. Even passengers in trains shot buffalo through the windows.

The Cheyenne, Arapaho, and Sioux tribes sometimes attacked the Union Pacific workers who laid tracks across their territory, so the government hired Pawnee Indians to protect the workers. Soon the workers themselves carried guns for protection. The Plains Indians eventually had to allow the railroad to come through their land.

Towns began to pop up along the tracks. They had train depots, repair shops, and temporary lodging for workers. Cheap buildings quickly went up, including stores, **saloons**, restaurants, and other businesses. These towns had reputations for attracting criminals. One city was described as "the wickedest city in America." Another town averaged 1 murder a day. Often when the workers moved on, the cities were torn down or abandoned. Sometimes, new settlers moved in and built up permanent towns like Cheyenne, Wyoming, named after the Cheyenne Indians.

When Europeans first arrived in North America, there were an estimated 15 to 60 million buffalo in the West. By the end of the 1800s, only about 1,000 were left.

RACE TO THE END

At the end of 1867, the Union Pacific had laid 400 more miles (644 km) of track than the Central Pacific, which had lost much time going through the Sierra Nevada during winter. Each company still had over 500 miles (805 km) of track to lay before reaching its destination in Utah.

The Union Pacific had a last-minute conflict about its final route. Company vice president Thomas Durant wanted the final route built through Salt Lake City, Utah, which was the home of one of the company's most important stockholders, Brigham Young. The Union Pacific chief engineer, Grenville Dodge, believed this route was a waste of time and only meant to bring more money to Durant. The Republican nominee for president, Ulysses S. Grant, was asked to settle the disagreement. He sided with Dodge.

In March 1869, 50 miles (80 km) separated the companies and the meeting point of Promontory Summit, Utah. The 2 companies began competing to see which could lay the most track in a single day. Durant bet Charles Crocker, who oversaw the workers of the Central Pacific, $10,000 that he could not break the previous Union Pacific record of 8 miles (13 km) in 1 day. On April 28, 1869, a small team of Chinese and Irish Central Pacific workers laid over 10 miles (16 km) of track in 1 day.

After it was decided that the best route for the transcontinental railroad would be north of Salt Lake City, Young protested in Washington. However, even after the government and both railroads supported this route, Young continued to provide the Union Pacific with workers and supplies.

the Central Pacific workers averaged 4,400
et per hour, how many hours did it take to
omplete 10 miles? Convert the total distance
 feet: 1 mile is equal to 5,280 feet.

= the number of hours

  5,280 feet
×   10 miles
52,800 feet

et up a proportion: $\dfrac{feet}{hours} = \dfrac{feet}{hours}$

$\dfrac{400}{1} = \dfrac{52,800}{h}$

$\dfrac{400\,h}{4,400} = \dfrac{52,800}{4,400}$ (Reminder: You can cross out zeroes.)

$= \dfrac{528}{44}$

$\begin{array}{r} 12 \\ 4)\overline{528} \\ -44 \\ \hline 88 \\ -88 \\ \hline 0 \end{array}$

= 12 hours

e men finished in 12 hours.

Brigham Young

The Railroad Legacy

The Central Pacific reached its end point before the Union Pacific, but the end of the race was only the start of the celebration. Officials from both companies traveled to the ceremony to join the 2 sets of tracks. The last 2 rails were carried by teams of Chinese and Irish workers. A golden spike was made for the occasion. Company leaders Thomas Durant and Leland Stanford tapped in the last spike to connect the 2 lines. The West and East coasts were now connected by rail and by the telegraph line that had been constructed alongside it.

During the following years, the railroad changed many lives in the United States. A person could travel across the country in 1 week for $65. Before the railroad, the trip took several months and cost close to $1,000. Mail cost just pennies a letter and arrived in a few days, compared to the weeks and dollars spent before.

Today, there are several transcontinental railroads across the United States. Trains are still the best way to ship many goods long distances, and many people believe they are the best way to see the different lands of the United States. People today are still thinking of ways to improve transportation. As they do this, they define and solve problems using proportions, much like those used in this book. Keep solving problems, and perhaps one day you will make history like the builders of the first transcontinental railroad!

GLOSSARY

assembly line (uh-SEHM-blee LYN) A way of putting together a product in a factory by moving it along a line of workers. Each worker performs the same task over and over. They add or adjust a part of the product until the job is finished.

bankrupt (BANK-rupt) The state of being unable to pay debts and of having property legally taken over for payment of these debts.

bond (BAHND) A certificate representing a loan that must be paid back with interest.

discriminate (dis-KRIH-muh-nayt) To treat some people better than others without any fair reason.

equation (ih-KWAY-zhuhn) A statement of the equality of 2 mathematical expressions.

isthmus (IHS-muhs) A narrow strip of land that connects 2 land areas.

locomotive (loh-kuh-MOH-tihv) A self-propelled vehicle that pulls railroad cars.

Mormon (MOHR-muhn) A follower of a form of Christianity founded by Joseph Smith.

saloon (suh-LOON) A bar.

stagecoach (STAYJ-cohch) A horse-drawn passenger and mail coach that runs on a regular schedule between established stops.

terrain (tuh-RAYN) The physical features of an area of land.

INDEX